D1194364

Casting Sequences

CASTING

SEQUENCES

POEMS BY

MARJORIE WELISH

THE UNIVERSITY OF GEORGIA PRESS

ATHENS AND LONDON

Published by the University of Georgia Press
Athens, Georgia 30602
© 1993 by Marjorie Welish
All rights reserved

Designed by Betty Palmer McDaniel
Set in ten on thirteen Palatino
by Tseng Information Systems, Inc.
Printed and bound by Thomson-Shore, Inc.
The paper in this book meets the guidelines for
permanence and durability of the Committee on
Production Guidelines for Book Longevity of the
Council on Library Resources.

Printed in the United States of America

97 96 95 94 93   C   5 4 3 2 1

97 96 95 94 93   P   5 4 3 2 1

Library of Congress Cataloging in Publication Data
Welish, Marjorie, 1944–
Casting sequences : poems / by Marjorie Welish.
        p.   cm.
ISBN 0-8203-1511-7 (alk. paper).
— ISBN 0-8203-1512-5 (pbk. : alk. paper)
I. Title.
        PS3573.E4565C37   1993
811'.54—dc20   92-27609
                            CIP

British Library Cataloging in Publication Data available

To
BARBARA GUEST
and
HARRY MATHEWS

Acknowledgments

The author and publisher gratefully acknowledge the
following publications in which these poems first appeared:

Conjunctions: "Danbury, Connecticut," "Design, with Drawing,"
"For Four Violins," "Grace's Tree, I," "Kiss Tomorrow Goodbye"
Denver Quarterly: "Hymn to Life to Cliff, I, VI"
Infolio: "Hymn to Life to Cliff, II"
Sulfur: "Casting Sequences," "Scalpel in Hand," "Twenty-three
Modern Stories"
Talisman: "As Though Through a Tunnel," "Grace's Tree, II"

StellaR Graphics/Collectif Generation published "Krater, I" and
"Krater, II" in *Boîtes à Malices*, Paris, 1992.
Finally, the author wishes to thank the New York Foundation for
the Arts for a grant enabling her to write this book.

Contents

CASTING SEQUENCES

Twenty-three Modern Stories

                              Perpetually roughed up
by the dawdling, blushing drone of an airplane,

"the viola with a restrained, sometimes" restringing
made the plunge
                    upon these planks
because of all the shores that must be visited.

". . . and continuities, whose intersections"
spreading hot wax
                         on privation
and on the phrase "this text,"
                                   united once again,
are inescapably drawn toward the open door.

The bells have ceased altogether.
"The air bit hard and cold"
                         spaced in such a way as to make a triad
of arrangements thus:
                         old and tired star, guitar and protean
interdisciplinary soprano.

Casting Sequences

A page dramatically estranged, nor lacking
$$\qquad\qquad\qquad$$ bombardment out of sync
with the event that
$$\qquad\qquad\qquad$$ annihilated into sudden pianissimo
a few songs.
$$\qquad\qquad$$ Where death is naked to the waist
in radiance,
$$\qquad\qquad$$ and sudden extension
piloted across a vocal line
$$\qquad\qquad\qquad$$ finds an event,
the page lies still, a chaotic catchall of springtime.

Alphabetizing the cards
$$\qquad\qquad\qquad$$ slavishly
the person comes first,
$$\qquad\qquad\qquad$$ in cold blood
and spelled out . . .
$$\qquad\qquad$$ "pale and enfeebled by the remoteness"
of actuality.
$$\qquad\qquad$$ Of actual number, pale
and spelled in cold,
$$\qquad\qquad\qquad$$ a person is impeturbably
alphabetizing cards
$$\qquad\qquad$$ torn from himself,
casting from himself riddle and raven,
$$\qquad\qquad\qquad$$ riddle and reticule.
Mildew
$$\qquad$$ "of adjacent realities"

and recurrent themes

                              and recursive themes,
assisting the physics of a sinking fastball or aerodynamic
stall—speculative,

                    half-visible—and all talking at once,
the only such televised

                         obliquities in which
the elite and public are exactly coincident

                                        and lifted up.
To get livelier,

                to accelerate the unridable lift,
the only such televised praxis, half-visible

                                    breaking pitches
wince—

          and they all remark on it,

                              they all recur
in the slower moving air.

Design, with Drawing

1

And slowly, Monet underwent a conversion from wrist
to shoulder and thence to the ambit
of paint dragged across surface unappeased:

                        plasticity without an appointment
or trace of retinal light.

Unimpressed, an editor asks, "Was Pollock even seen
standing before this canvas opining 'Monet,'
Monet, ceasing to exist, I want to paint like you?"

Apparition. Really, I swear it.

                    And wearying.

And slowly. And somewhere other than observable water.

2

                    A mossy bank, schoolgirlish.

Of lacunae passing through literal mentalities
a few pages later.

                  A parapet, an undercurrent

of misplaced exactitude these odysseys transcended.
Why ask the artist? Ask the art:

              rock-ribbed

breakwater, to mark the hue and cry of forgetfulness
and gray areas.

Addressees,

what constitutes evidence in stylistic transmission?
Disbelief "much bigger and faster"

or problems corroborated,

in a more efficient axe.

Kiss Tomorrow Goodbye

1

Among us are those who apply
dysfunctional tactics to convened ordinariness
of setting, as in certain booby-trapped stories.

For similar reasons,
a narrative complete with lunch menu and
    stereoscopic thugs . . . ,
complete with cigarette yet for all that a narrative clad in
    itself . . . ,
or a ventriloquist and dummy, minus the ventriloquist . . . ,
all threaten the logical unit.

Complete with cigarette
yet disturbing the infinitesimal trash, the depiction,
this ventriloquist set a bowler-hatted dummy
on one knee, served up a twin
on the other.

                    Thus translated,
and torn limb from limb, "naively,"
the rivers ran
and Osiris spread showering selves, showering down
existence after death.

2

Death served up a twin
the rivers ran
limb from limb
trash the depiction

minus the depiction
as in certain booby-trapped stories
for similiar reasons
narrative clad in itself
on one knee
on the other
convened ordinariness
complete with cigarette.

Moses und Aron

Entirety.
Inquiry.

Sunken revelation
minus the idolatry

and bacchanalian click-track:
where is ought?

Schönberg asks of this mien,
of this cabinet

impaired to shed light.

Entirety somehow annulled
qualitatively through inquiet,

optimum warmth. Anathema
corresponding to gold

mimesis,
mind. Where is rival

dumbfoundedness?

The entirety hammering outside
the fool.

An appeal to
sounding that note.

You were omniscient a moment ago.
To beguile many and be beguiled by one

incompatibility.
Why?

Schönberg asks.
Screams, laughter, silences.

Do you wish to escape without saving this page?

Dumbfoundedness?
discolored now in laughter.

Screams, laughter where there is enigma or the onset of
    nearby,
discolored now,

disinterred many times as they parody ultramarine,
the sun, the sun's disappearance.

Move What? To Where?
Unimaginable, omnipresent, eternal,

stay far from us,
Move What? *Staff, law; serpent, wisdom.* To Where?—*Now this
    God can be imagined.*

Scalpel in Hand

1

Let us effect a moratorium on things.

Let us say
an object is not an image, aerodynamically speaking.

Let us say
"Speak, or be silent."

Let us legislate
"the sound elements in a spoken language."

For argument's sake,
let us say the craze for black
may be dazed with shape, size, and color of commodity.

For argument's sake,
the flutter of nearby bleeding does not render a charcoal
    lemon tragic,
although tragedy eclipsed by subject matter
may be eligible for illustration by Grandville;
"an object is not an image."
Say the subtly bled shape does not induce suffering in
    lemons, however
blackened, however centrally massed the putative anguish.
Let us legislate anguish,
let us say "anguish" in unison very loud.
In a spoken language, syllables are extinguished
once gathered by the silhouette dissembling death.

2

In the center, rays from the sun and much still life
denied body, denied pantomime
and yet much language whenever and wherever

land radii. Abstract and sanitary bodilessness.
If no evidence, if no physionomic
ignition, then just what does the author mean?

In conversation with the author, find
a charcoal axis drawn *soto voce*, denied body,
denied yet blurting out whatever unjustly perishable

sacrifice or contingency,
much ostension of cipher
and rays of the sun.

3

An object is not an image,
aerodynamically speaking.
Verblessness in space
reserving passive
rather than active tawdriness
of those sparse
accoutrements in free fall.
In this falling through painted
representation, object and image:
snails versus "snails'
genitals in the form of stars,"
depending on how we construe
the symbolic
vanishing magnitude.

In vanishing magnitude,
the symbolic.
Depending on our construal,
stars in exhaustion
and genitals suspended on a string.
Ephemera, illustrate this.
Free fall, illustrate this,
scalpel in hand,
in an acutely skeptical reading
of the snail incised with dotted
passivity in tawdriness,
the object obsolescent, abject or gone.
When is an object not an object?

Speak and Be Silent

A red plane, a blue
inclination raised above,

gathering the image,
smeared with process;

the object: the blue cube suffering
an unbounded administration of shape.

The drag on this plane is absolute,
the blue cube, five hours

spent, with fatigue perfected
and operating three-dimensionally.

Speak and be silent,
perfection being realized

in the realism companiably athwart
whitewash ("merely whitewashed"

substance). This is it:
imagine dismantling a tissue,

now imagine a semblance
with absolutely no editorial prerogative.

HYMN TO LIFE TO CLIFF

Hymn to Life to Cliff

I

1

Of juniper bushes chafing against the earth,
some melodious plot or politics
having been permitted.

Of happiness passing into unhappiness,
of juniper bushes chafing against
political stagecraft.

Of happiness passing,
of happiness chafing against an utterance
of iron filings attached to the goat's iris

in exactitude, wherein grief
mistrusts every pretense
pictured through the apparatus of black,

of tragedy,
art listing decidedly.
Art is not all that is available to the eye.

A hairline fracture saunters up the rockface.

And in the grass are small wild crocuses from hills goats
have cropped to barrenness.

2

It was doctrine shaping itself
in a life. As Berger tells it,

a farmer ridiculed for sentiment
in resisting the advent of debt,

preferring a plow
and cloud cover to tractor,

dramatized the engendered brown endangered
near the doorstep, in an argument

definitive of his position, vista
and mess, saying (at last),

"Technology is systemic,"
and so cast his lot against them.

3

Art listing decidedly.

Wild incarnation and goat
in a tendency to confuse
generous combat
erase
brilliantly

excerpts
iris
other

theory
ravaged
other

the concealed cash reserves
of wild crocuses.

II

1

And in the barrens where burial is
a static situation, small wild iris,

often inimical,
astygmatic,

art listing decidedly
Oedipus.

Art is not all available to the eye
if we ask ourselves the right questions . . .

2

The conscious existence of men in their life processes
without saying a word. A peasant opening the fastening
bolt of the press, argues the ideology well enough,
Berger would maintain, as does the tax on the residuum
of fruit squeezed, young liquid running out.

3

On
as
or
in
off
is.

Of juniper bushes chafing sympathetically—
I cannot believe a delusional theory helps us.

III

1

Stubbornness increases his suffering but is not
the cause of it. His suffering accelerated.
His suffering increased; stubbornness smiled upon it.
Like us or not, like him. Unrelenting
roulette adores his suffering, a form of because
increasingly a gambler's fallacy.
His suffering dropped into a flaming pit;
stubbornness smiled upon it. Like probability
so variable as to be freakish, his suffering increased;
it did not cease to be. His suffering skipped ahead,
clambered up occupational scarcity.
Stubbornness made bold his foretold oblivion.
Then there is the "happy ending"
of cliff where the blunt goat is penciled in.

2

To assume determinism from foreknowledge is fallacious
yet effective drama depends on it.

3

Is value increasing
adjacency between grooves,
nebeneinander ineluctably
against a backdrop
of hellenizing
offhandedness?

IV

1

Some melodious plot or politics; politics or plot did
    not cease.
His suffering animated the thistledown, caressed the
    apparatus.
Of happiness passing, on unhappiness and other matters
of grief, of tragedy and its counterfeits.
"It was a tragic loss" o'erstrides the tabloids, spoils the page,
seeps through the vellum, dominates the palimpsest
of calamitous acts. A sad aggregate
of stubble poking through snowy tar, mashed under
    tarpaulins, snowy.
The coziness of entailment: if winter, can spring be far?
A hairline fracture saunters up the rock face.
And in the grass are small wild crocuses from hills goats
have cropped to barrenness, have razed.

2

Remarkable are the propensities effected between words
    and deeds,
the words being, as Lynette Hunter has said in another
    context,
the materiality of belief.

3

Lupine and trillium
also included bilingually

liminal time
and everywhere gray

except for cawing
seizing the edge

of atrophy
and going on for a hundred verses.

V

1

The crisis: dubious cylinders in intolerant

productivity weighed against agrarian improvement,

his heart prolonging the open disability for a while.

Peristalsis has stopped during this procedure.

———————

To write a tragedy of history rather than a tragedy of myth
or perhaps a tragic myth occurring *in illo tempore*

beneath the juniper grief in ratcheted cry
the reverberating tractor subtending grief

machinery always stands ready to engulf the irrecoverable
in the circuitry of here and now, gasoline among the
    imperatives

dramaturgical circuitry draws its energy from trenchant
    critique
the common wheel comes around stubbornly

exploring the thematic potential of uncathartic black
like a submersible design in the adventures of a diver.

———————

Why this tax on love?
this exacting tribute, this tax
the more exacting, the more incapacitated

in illo tempore beneath the juniper
in such a time, of such vernacular
eras beneath these events

wrestled with the explosive vigilance
quiet taken to the mat, the volatile square
of equal justice. Voluntary windowlessness

of the linguistic substratum.
The quiet ventilated
in the first festival of vigilance.

2

Permanently recurring retributive contours
obsess the plot, to stop
the smooth fastening bolt from opening and closing
according to need. More and more, the inspector intercepts
the works. The litigious figure is summed up, rapidly.

3

If something happens at random . . .
I mean, a negative one . . .

VI

1

Of happiness passing into unhappiness,
of juniper bushes chafing against corrosive

matter breathing out heavily
in the ram—yet calamity is not enough

barrenness, although the wicked, piteous
chafing against the chthonic part of the idea
sustains the sweat on his face.
With possibly more averse

irremediable gradient in which
you and I are hesistant, the sense of
deletion in the same body
is that for which we today give thanks.

Intensity in the response
wrested from the harrow
is a fulfillment, prophetic

and, with luck, more than piteous.
With possibly further ancient
irremediable deletion than obtains

our daily rearrangement,
the sense of a tragic choice to be made
is that for which we today give thanks.

2

The theory of tragedy, in this view, does not separate
actor and spectator but extends indefinitely to the farmer
walking behind his plough, who drags behind him his
plough of automated encroachment; now, unspoken drifts
of his ploughed resistance intensify the parable of
spreading agribusiness in present-day France. With
muddy experiments in process, and a style accelerating in
tactical ellipsis, utterances alight abdominally: a limb—is

it yours?—held between thumb and forefinger, the arable
area of ideologies he had experienced moves in on him in
self-evidence, in Spandex, and in newer ways of
disappearance.

3

Black square trapdoor, prewar
deathlessness, or are we falling up,
unhappy equestrian. As if of learning,

envy contingent upon hope
written here, even as
"goat" crisscrosses "tragedy"

elsewhere. Unhappy equestrian, art is not
molting now. Rebuffed shapelessness
attracts and repels,
involves erroneous (desired) limits,

yet it might turn.
                            An inscription
asks for a delayed verdict—
a stumbling block.
                            Black trapdoor,

or are we falling up, unhappy equestrian?

IF I BLINDFOLD YOU

Glance

Courtesies through the way,
the ways in which the thought, the thoroughfare
funneled thoroughly, might rush to awaken "nature,"
no fewer than sixty meanings for the long race, heroes at
  the close . . .

Door reflected in drowned mirror
of a nonauditory kind—
how is it possible we underneath in serious weakness
exist accredited?

Monotonous mirroring appended below the drawing
of self-preoccupation to report, and in re-presenting
luggage to the closet. Excited ice skates and boxes
uncover "incompatible visibilities" occupying that space.

Surviving the stealth of her famous persona,
surviving a pitiable appetite for the cruel nocturne
is your unabbreviated worthwhileness
indifferent to the subroutine alotted prearticulated hair, teeth
  and nails . . .

The Poetry Project

A wave tangled up in itself, as though antirational
and loving the ungrammaticalities, the matted
information making no sense. Who was it
who accomplished the disenchantment
of the phrase, any phrase in ease of our being
yet especially that of the unattended green
municipality admonishing us for arriving
"without leashes"? Traveling the distance, as organza
trapped in ice or as silhouettes vexed
inordinately until ultimately some thing-in-itself
delayed beyond what is meant and this
untitled sack. Between parentheses is that
whatever perfectly adapted to the hand—

or lies slumbering with amendments
as our steps drag behind yours, dropping off
behind your occupancy. Like rain in shadow
yet pertaining to you, *a song of prudence.*

As Though Through a Tunnel

. . . as though through a tunnel absorbing its "disincarnated"
shadow in an exemplary escape to canvas,
of canvas in wilderness and with characteristic candor
of yellow, slammed onto a circumference
of "joy, glory, and love," three sites rewriting the eye's
consensual criteria.
              Not claustrophobia but fear of paradigm shift,
hanging heavily in the studio, I said of visitors'
    exterminating
impatience. It collects
reconciled to differing vocabularies, enshrined in difference
without being named as such.

Enshrined in vocabularies of reprisal:
as though through surface "stripped of its prerogative to
    assume,"
as though through somatic extremity, white on white,
as though through a chrysalis of undifferentiated childish
    misgivings.

Subscriptions, most spontaneous ones, generated a folklore.
A poetics had been withdrawn from that thing.
Cantering into a caveat or sacrifice . . .

Hydra-headed

With sight unseen
or severed yesterday, partitioned
into delicate
dispossession of sleep.

A line of pervasive sleep
perfectly illustrates rereading
the meridians you spoke of,
warned us of.

Pulling out all stops and swinging a bat at here and at there,
he lowers the phrase "There is," of which sleeplessness is
of orchestral aspect, in the middle distance walk the couple,
the phrase "There is."

As though from anywhere
and/or of orchestral aspect, this shadow in duplicate,
or more shadow, histrionically.
Tetrahedra

hydra-headed, about to
freeze light, sunder 3-D into 2-D brilliantly.
There appear certain silhouettes in consequence of this:
a couple walking in middle distance.

Of this ostensive felt-tip
and name in measurement, set next to "F,"
a.k.a. "figure," apparently.
See figure in side panel.

Serving suggestion: strawberries on toast. Strawberries?!
Over the intercom came the call:
Will all the red things and pink things in the world line up
by size? Taste, a simple tidiness settling on the eye's social
edifice.

If I Blindfold You

Remnants of counterclockwise.
Remnants of inclement tardiness.

Elephants are equidistant,
are irreversible.

If I blindfold you and take you into the kitchen . . .
Navigational path

past and present
hyacinth

following a given brawl downstream,
narrating an episode of patrimony.

———————

Remnants of tardiness, very sweet.
And soft are remnants of tardiness.

Through the mountain pass came the outermost species,
elephants empowering Hannibal, astride the mountain pass.

If I blindfold you and take you into your kitchen . . .
While in your familiar kitchen, you could be blind and not
    know it.

Throw one's weight into the scale
of a) associative b) not associative temperatures, be they in
    words, images or diagrams,

following a given brawl downstream,
following it upstream to patrimony.

Impenetrable to others,
those cubical forms in coral.

Because we must add
a chastening bruise

to stark abstemiousness of order, of orders
we assume for a moment the necessity of it

semiparalyzed
or gathered via Ionian shyness

to fall across the porch of incorrigible states
and upon the sentence set within

a song or hymn in praise of gladness:
"Let us wipe away any incapacity in our mark!"

————————

Wishing to make metaphysical plaster
Wishing to be a matrix.

To this we must add a chastening bruise
It has come to our attention . . . a chastening thought

assuming the designation "pain"
to refer to certain prolific

fissures commencing in the present, in presences
of mental states, stageworthy

once paralyzed rather than thought through thoroughly.
Since not given to thought, paralysis prompts our plan

of nonidentical yet necessarily correlated colonnades—
our thickened entitites, as with a sentence, our sentence
    in antis

or anthem that wipes away any servility
in the epistemic realm.

Bodiless, Bodiless in Translation, I

The forest wetting its lips.
A flight of steps and naked perspectives
seen unburdening themselves in the chill
details of the analysis.

The aforesaid speech
playing across an amphitheater in the woods
like an unlikely couple meeting under artificial
    circumstances—
the saplings that grow from stone are the actors now.

———————

In a much quoted passage,
desire warbles a surfeit of messages throughout the
    commemorative woods
whose meaning in amphitheater presents ourselves to
    ourselves.

Many, often divergent flora are in delicate competition
and a little published,
as when a phrase I speak awakes as yours.

Bodiless, Bodiless in Translation, II

Of meaning and halting
discrepancy in a mirror afloat
under fully fledged foliage
being dragged into occasion,

as I hope I have shown.
"At love's entreaty,"
nonsense most aggressively,
and under advisement.

––––––––––

"That surface is cut into again"
eloquently, the palm
and halting discrepancy in a mirror
perpendicular to foliage

do there embrace.
Authors, then, are menaced
by carnivalesque dirty work
thou had less deserved.

Bodiless, Bodiless in Translation, III

Literature from the start
deleting the sun, or inserting another intentionality
of time, whose wristwatch you first created,
sweeps across the eclipse of vicious hornets
surmounting the three tombs.

Allow widows and orphans?
Their energies consume themselves, as an even darker night
    or document
renounces the unnaturally bright face indicative of an
    indestructible sunset,
celestial repagination
correlating events of two types.

————————

As one proceeds,
the average typist situated in space
is spurred on by the unnaturally bright deletion
of numerals, expressed exactly the same as content believed.

Using hard spaces
of air corridors preserved by flying birds,
or of reluctance,
functioning as a lack in the capacity of an inspired
    omission . . .

Danbury, Connecticut

While winter remains without shadow
that brings lasting credit, it insinuates
that the amphitheater inserts new

birdcalls—a burst almost, strafing the upper
slow latency. And still,
and straitened. In this going abroad

the solid observer antecedes the rebirth
of space. Yet, another voice breaks,
then successively

new excrescences of the invisible
aural spectacle move a process
well in advance of seeing.

———————

Advance or gather, then,
self-improvement
in statistical error
focal length
evangelical furlough
social fabric
time study
quarter-tone melodies.

As list differs from lyric,
so, too, these growing pains:
First railroad from Danbury
to South Norwalk opens in 1851.

Here, take this
catgut and wire
crushed green glass
bitonal suspension bridge
slam-bang melodeon
of some sporadic good.

That the air's centralized indeterminacy inserts new
birdcalls—a burst almost, in the upper
mid-range,

in the upper portion of the portrayal
of vocal coagulation.

Acting on things: "I reproached him a thousand times."

Felt to Be Planetary

Beneath the hill of daylight
are upper reaches where halogen is preparing
the volume of relaxation imagined
gold. *Lumière fluorescente.*

A resident alarmist.
My two weimaraners, Fear and Loathing.
No such thing,
to mention my normal examples, Kenneth.

As light-filling whiteness
breathed terribly cool, there lay open a caliphate
of cool white fluorescent light fixtures inhaling
and augmenting

daylight in mint condition.
Daylight, its nature and purpose.
How do you know? inheres in the area
you replace with criteria of forgetfulness.

Of this 60-cycle residential hum, retinal
nature in the artist's possession
and a relatively unaffected green, naïve really.
New York 1964, Green Gallery.

In pursuant to mint condition
is light, platitudinous, we call the Theory of No Theory.
A girl with two cows, how do you know?
inheres remorselessly in the close or lane.

Inexistent.
Forget it.
No such thing.
A resident alarmist.

"Just the story,"
said the dramaturge, in assured pursuit
of transparency there,
yet implicative with Anton Pavlovich

is that of A forever drifting toward A',
hanging a condition to be raised, lowered,
a condition of wonderment enervated, or whatever
avatar of "is" can float.

A Twinkle in His Eye

In mint condition is day through day, pink and daylight
fluorescent lamps revising sluggish if shining
silverware. A ceiling-recessed downlight

quietly monopolizes the eye, in effect, a light
"not like a ceiling but like the underside
of a hurricane." And in this laboratory of low-brightness

incandescence, daylight is a detriment
to ballets of dimness and large areas
of uneliminated white dresses. Readying a soffit

that was gently luminous is light in likeness
fastening its halogens on the light heavyweight.
Unprecedented happiness, deducing pink light

from a chandelier of international scope, lit
and enjoying green neon genitalia
slightly launched against the low-brightness

incandescent street lamps: look, look
toward the ceiling-recessed vision, its downlight,
down and eyeing the immaculate alignment of daylight and
    cool white
fluorescent light where sunshine is in lift-off.

Grace's Tree, I

When did you discover you've an abstract mind? Playing
　　with blocks
even as others were playing with sheep, contending with
　　accidents
upon this earth and balkanization within a two-dimensional
　　meadow,
the two-dimensional meadow against which and through
　　which salient
facts draw at least part of their sustenance.

Threading the adjusted grove on the right-hand side,
I stayed to play with blocks procedurally, madly in love,
and in a magical moment,
capsized the puzzle to turn smiling faces into pervasiveness,
the pervasiveness of those geometric schemes.

Farming the torrid difficulties,
faced with abhorrent difficulties on the obverse of
　　agricultural stress
and seeking medicinal solutions to power,
once a farmer, now political activist—you, spurned by
　　likeness
are nonetheless remembered by literati.

Given your considerable accoustical acuity, facility
　　even, reach
more complexity than is readily accessed by your
　　wanderlust,
your carelessness,
as when the sheep farmer you once were asked of his pallid
　　colleagues: now just what
satisfactorily invites the geology of the situation?

Now just what sovereign geology accessed by your
   wanderlust
capsized the puzzle to turn the smiling faces into
   pervasiveness
like the grove on the right-hand side of the gravely
   assymetrical situation
against which and through which salient facts draw at least
   part of their sustenance?

Grace's Tree, II

Without leaving that space, a sentence's
disinterment is causing sensation
and signs: like rustic sighs in the grove of an
    unordinary kind
of basket, lacking right-handedness to feed from her hand.

To play with blocks profusely, through subtraction
or to telephone only to receive
an algorithm straightaway, as you handed over the receiver
to Shirl, illuminated cognitively,

and gratefully, who, now awakened and taking a left,
pleads your considerable accoustic acuity to the
    agriculturalist
no less diminuitive and illuminated in lapis
adumbrating even more lamb.

Given the manner in which
companions help him to his feet again to hand him his
    common fatigue
accessed indiscriminately within a blue field,
it is no wonder the incumbent asked his pallid colleagues:
    now just

what can still explain the sleeping youth, so diminuitive
in a forwarded letter or algorithm you handed
only to receive
right-handedness feeding from her hand.

Grace's Tree, III

Companions helped him to his feet again and handed him
   his common fatigue.
The most obvious (but by no means only) attribute: leaning.
As for textural features, aquiline and firm assonance contests
   the sense,
with its partial echo and biases concealing further
   passageways.

Companions help him to his feet again, one using a heavy
   stick as a lever,
while his laughing befrienders decide what a simple concept
   is: vanilla
incapable of being seen, or gray entirety. Yet related
and indebted to these is gray entirety set within gray
   extension.

Helping him to his feet again, companions stood fast in the
   eddying
sublunary domain under varying historical conditions.
" 'Whose kid? Our kid!' came cries from the crowd as
   women wept and men
muttered angrily and people surged forward to touch the
   motorcade."

Companions helped him to his feet again. As a rule such
   reinterpretations
get the thing done. People go naked, or clad in skins.
A forest fire can be seen astutely ravaging the woods later
   resurrected
as hordes of stories destined for a room arranged like this.

Of stories destined for a room, that eddying sublunary
    domain yielding
cries from the crowd while laughing befrienders decide what
    a simple
concept is, there is one told about using a lever against
    fatigue
with its partial echo and biases concealing further
    passageways.

OF A DISPLAY

To J.M.
who provoked it

Nowhere More Vivid

Fatigue *or my tired breath*
Touch me not *or the evil hour*
Illuminate *light to my pleasure*
Cold comfort *frost and shade.*

Extradition *drives out the shadows*
Baronial *and the other plume*
Interiority *carries within*
Lullaby *consoling Heaven.*

Michelangelesque

Only our noon *or my tired breath*
Of ruined evening *or the evil hour*
Named by rival *light to my pleasure*
Defends morning *in frost and shade.*

Perpetual morning *drives out the shadows;*
Contracts, letters, *and the other plume*
Of ever-executed noon *carry within*
These signatures of *consoling Heaven.*

————————

Fire took no thought *or my tired breath*
Wet that day *or the evil hour*
Denying fire*light to my pleasure*
With rain lost *in frost and shade.*

Hurled earth *drives out the shadows*
Unrolling mares' tails, *and the other plume*
In which wake of earth *carries within*
The non-finito, air's *consoling Heaven.*

————————

Air unembellished *or my tired breath*
Stagnates: infanticide *or the evil hour.*
Therapeutic *light to my pleasure*
Unlikely in self-disclosed *frost and shade.*

Saintly utility *drives out the shadows*
Of specious good *and the other plume*
Lit confusingly, *carried within.*
Down from your pedestal, *consoling Heaven!*

Suppressed Misfortunes

"Suppressed misfortunes have a double strength."
—MICHELANGELO

Breath tired my or *or my tired breath*
Hour evil the or *or the evil hour*
Pleasure my to light *light to my pleasure*
Shade and frost in *in frost and shade.*

Shadows the out drives *drives out the shadows*
Plume other the and *and the other plume*
Within carries *carries within*
Heaven consoling *consoling Heaven.*

———————

Breathing out *or my tired breath*
Hour unpalatable *or the evil hour*
Himself his abacus *light to my pleasure*
Or muddle, tonal *in frost and shade.*

Driven shadows *drives out the shadows*
Ephemeral bounty or *the other plume*
Carries within *carries within*
Contentment, *consoling Heaven.*

Lace unraveling *or my tired breath*
The problematic *or the evil hour*
Thread, threading *light to my pleasure*
In frost. I, *in frost and shade.*

A system of knots *drives out the shadows*
Almost to a man. *And the other plume*

Unable to die *carries within*
A sampler in cirrus, *consoling Heaven.*

———————

These intervals *or my tired breath,*
fallow throughout *the evil hour*
Of spirit. *Light to my pleasure;*
Light to my labor *in frost and shade.*

Design *drives out the shadows.*
Visibility, status *and the other plume*
Of similiar worldliness *carry within*
The sumptuary unction of *consoling Heaven.*

———————

Of information *or my tired breath*
The merely literal *or evil hour*
Ordering and insouciant *light to my pleasure:*
Verse, incurious *in frost and shade.*

Astonishment *drives out the shadows*
Of facticity *and the other plume.*
Or is it conception *carried within*
Incessant meriting, *Consoling Heaven?*

Of a Display

Restoration *can be all boredom and anxiety,*
artifice *the only remedy.*
Cast *among us there is nothing human*
alive. *The heart, the mind, the soul will then*
cleanse *the evil of all error*
and *the first and the second death drive out*
resemblance *in my fate.*

Restoration botched *can be all boredom and anxiety.*
Plexiglas broadly discussed *the only remedy*
cast *among us; there is nothing human*
alive. *The heart, the mind, the soul will then*
become more apparent, if not elaborate. *The evil of all error*
and *the first and the second death drive out*
material somewhat feigned *in my fate.*

Ut pictura poesis *can be all boredom and anxiety.*
Euphronios Plexiglas, *the only remedy*
for piecing the vast schematic *among-us-there-is-nothing-human*
    mixing bowl. *The heart, the mind, the soul will then*
liquify *the evil of all error*
with commentary: *distain and anger*
belonging to a sphere as *the first and the second death drive out*
the literal mind.

Continuous service *can be all boredom and anxiety.*
Nonsequitur *the only remedy,*
and with plastic *amongst us there is nothing human.*
Leave without pay. *The heart, the mind, the soul will then*
exchange *the evil of all error* for plastic armature,
leaving behind these volutes of *distain and anger.*

In faulty semesters *the first and the second death drive out*
unceasing surface. Refocus this controversy, enclose.

Repairing the whole *can be all boredom and anxiety;*
support beyond pretense *the only remedy.*
Of the supplement *among us, there is nothing human*
supplying *the heart. The mind, the soul will then*
disrupt, not echo, *the evil of all error,*
and toward any but difference feel *distain and anger.*
Cast from elsewhere. *The first and the second death drive out*
historicizing lip and foot *in my fate.*

Faux marbre *can be all boredom and anxiety.*
Museological augery *the only remedy*
for lost material—*among us there is nothing human*
restored. *The heart, the mind, the soul will then*
imitate this material inadequacy.
The evil of all error cannot fail to impress.
Distain and Anger eating a peach.
The first and the second death
drive out natural phenomena *in my fate.*

Clay things *can be all boredom and anxiety,*
plastic infinitely recumbant, *the only remedy.*
Among us there is nothing human
. . . *the heart, the mind, the soul will then*
not sire sense impressions . . . *the evil of all error*
. . . *distain and anger*
. . . *the first and the second death drive out*
symmetry *in my fate.*

. . . *can be all boredom and anxiety*
plastic sepulchre, entirely his . . . *the only remedy*
. . . *among us there is nothing human*
. . . *the heart, the mind, the soul will then*

. . . the evil of all error
. . . distain and anger
. . . the first and the second death drive out
. . . in my fate.

Krater, I

Plastic,
a voiceless chassis
from which material has abstained,
remains uncorrupted by plausibility,
vying with clay,
that *returns and returns*
yields as if lowly, portable
dolor and pain.

Even before it breaks . . . *can be all boredom and anxiety*
skeptically at odds . . . *the only remedy*
own lips unexpectedly broken . . . *among us there is*
  nothing human
insofar as . . . *the heart, the mind, the soul will then*
posture . . . *the evil of all error*
was never so endowed, in doubt . . . *disdain and anger*
. . . *the first and the second death drive out*
. . . *in my fate.*

Krater, II

In its boughs,
historical effacement expending much effort
of classicizing, in clay *for thy dear beauty*
in clay-colored parody,
without deceiving yet without spark.

Is . . . *can be all boredom and anxiety,*
the museological . . . *the only remedy*
problem is that of surmise . . . *among us there is nothing human*
to complete . . . *the heart, the mind, the soul will then*
. . . *the evil of all error*
intentional . . . *disdain and anger*
. . . *the first and the second death drive out*
norms . . . *in my fate.*

FOR FOUR VIOLINS

Pre-echo

Pre-echo: Sound recorded so loud
that part of itself may magnetize adjacent windings

Twelve, thirteen, for two came wheeling down,
thirteen, for two darted about your eyes

interpreted as not knowing. A surname
is silenced. As in "tall, if sudden, groves"
or in "scuttled, sudden and tall,"
interpretations sewn into the unknown are those

we cannot substantiate. Physiognomy centrifugal,
Indo-European murmur gathering the sail
of the kind sailboat there, Igitur.
Mouth and ear are in centrifuge and unquiet.

Unquiet mouths would give more faithful
rendering of dissemination;
dissemination, ever an almost
perverse pleasure in translating tongues

in miasmas to the ear, through the ear.
Mental lakes close and correlated,
green lakes of filial piety
surely of, with and through the ear.

Torn from the ear obediently
this pieced entirety, in sepia
and insentient, a piece of which
lake is correlated to the ear.

A piece of the puzzle, rotated and blank,
in light pain,
the weight of existence
rotating the blank island,

chafing against the flesh inscape
of unjustified seeking.
Bleak notation for nostrils lower left
in regard of that flesh estuary

pressed from pulp and paper
for a perennial alphabet of lesser mortals—
primarily a thing to be read, you decided.
Select the size and face of type,

in 12-point figure-landscape, all exile
in these islands: dressed
companionable islands, dressed in phenomena.
Eclipse, exiling fullness. Irremissible,

irremissible solitude which constitutes a man.
Every visage, metalinguistic;
unblinking lakes in vague visage stretched across stretchers
which constitute a man.

Unblinking nonmimetic lakes taped to the cheek,
and here physiognomic truth-functions inhabit
a logically scented and nonspecific
self vindicated at all four corners, a kind of facial site.

Adrift in such skin, our iteration,
our iteration with which countries cannot vie, transliteration
    secretly abetting impenetrable baptism.
Portents of Rome, is this itinerant baptism abetting ours?
Adrift is the handkerchief

of which the paternity is known,
albeit threaded with thoroughly perplexed reference.
That blotted tongue, that thoroughly bollixed signature
    perplexing an anteriority
we cannot substantiate, this, despite known paternity.

Thirteen, for two darted about the eyes.
And the contingencies were attuned if irreducible;
attuned, if irreducible. And yet and yet.
Darting about the eyes, very near. In the darling eye.

For Four Violins

Many were fascinated with birth in erratic modes of
    construal. Meaning?
If keen on jazz, why, I asked did he borrow [the work of]
    Buxtehude? His name was Ben Paterson.
Ben, Fluxus.
From the start, we witnessed birth and death shadow forth a
    heterdox enrollment to replenish the situation.

Measureless, sayable without toil, were Robert Gorham
    Davis's reappearing myths.
His students found places near their neighbors of last week.
By habit, the student preferred the company of one she met
    by accident once.
Inclusive of retrograde thematics, the manifestation of Davis.

Records slipped from the book bag Ben had placed under
    his seat.
Flood, one of the varyingly weighted catastrophes itemized
    in Metaphor, Symbol and Myth, attracted a large
    following.
Habit tended to favor someone who with infrequent
    regularity plopped down a stack of LP's borrowed from the
    library.

Gather from time, and fourth generation variants,
    Buxtehude.
A natural situation sensibly represented in suitably receptive
    persons.
A natural vigilance sensibly represented.
Gather, from time and fourth generation variants, a phase
    elaborated with claim to plausibility.

In 1967, I heard a new release Ben wanted me to hear.
"What do you think?" he said. "Boring," I said. "Keep
   listening," he said.
"Now, what do you think?"
Steve Reich's new release, *Violin Phase*, interested Ben. He
   wanted me to hear it.

By habit we sat together.
A few notes rejuvenated when the new young god plays,
   when Paul Zukofsky's vigilant playing wore on.
Technique that elucidates process confers respect upon
   psychoaccoustic blur.
Common crystallizing devices such as the force of habit.

A minim of disenfranchisement.
"Boring," I said. "Keep listening," he said.
"What do you think?" he said. "Oceanic," I said.
A minim of anomie.

Drastic Measures

List names of persons.
With ski mask we approach the registrar.
Lacking imperative water, we staggered toward the registrar,
listing names of persons, dates of tenure.

Youth indicated
like a giant footprint;
the artist's imprimatur,
indicted. Such is youth.

An epistemological equivalent of hives or cystitis, indicating
  the ideological body is not well,
manages the volatile brew;
managing the brew, volatile and abundant
hives indicate our body.

You're impossible! All right, you're improbable.
An odor.
An odor rotating,
improbably you.

An odor shelved, or was it disallowed?
Stench in all singleness of heart,
a stench-filled room,
an odor of dereliction the library disallowed.

Whether malodorous people impinge
on others' rights
or the right of way
is an issue of free speech in some liberal resentment.

As we suffer a restaurant's good intentions,
odors, probabilities;
the new poets'
intentional restaurants.

At Princeton, the guys speak of restaurants
red,
feeling red—
the guys speaking of restaurants, the gals of intentionality,

as we did, as we might have done.
Feeling read
feeling read, an ontological claim said to inhere in the
    phenomenal
deeds we did, deeds we might have done.

Guitars and Tigers

Motionless against guy wires
across the loins in fixity,
to fix reference rather than to give meaning
or synonym for "guitar"

is "the length of S" designating the waxy
mentality plucked in leisure time;
time study: the study of work.
"The length of S" and "the length of S"

designating the same thing, waxing
this red. This red and that
wisp of red apprehension,
this in pursuant to directedness,

this business reply card.
"The length of S" designates a mention: Sloan-Kettering;
"The length of S" and "the length of S" and "the length
   of S,"
this, in exit

one meter long. Although a standard has no length,
the unmarked straightedge affixed there
refers now to a large Asian carnivore
having a tawny coat traversely striped with black.

Henry Cowell Plays the Standards

Science and Technology in Art Today
"These fragments I have shored . . ."

Modern American Usage
"From the steeples and mountains . . ."

To the Finland Station
The Poetics of Roman Ingarden

"I wandered lonely as a cloud . . ."
The Visionary Company

The arachnid in art, these spinnerets from which . . .
these fragments I have shored . . .
these fractions converted to a failure,
these spinnerets from which issue silk

"filament, filament, filament"
from steeples to mountains far from being perturbed,
far from being perturbed more perfectly
in a litany of casting forth of

silk and number, or accolade:
"which consists in touching the recipient's cheek with
     one's own"
in touching the recipient with one's own usage,
Modern American Usage,

in which "acquiesce" meets "assent."
Auxiliary vines are strangling our factory;

a wall indecipherable within the stranglehold of vine.
Acquiesce, meaning "assent" or "submit."

To the Finland Station, a destiny.
Overgrown would suggest nonutility
of chimneys or of a sensitive child.
This Way to the Waiting Room, go toward it but never attain

n-dimensional mentality. Throughout form-consciousness
strata come forth to upend curricula.
Nomenclature uncut. Strata come forth: Take courage!
In whatever alleged mentality, "valleys shall be raised up,
   and mountains made plain."

———————

These spinnerets from which issue failure drawn out
firm yet elastic, ductile
"till the ductile anchor hold"—
a finer technology in art, and he knew it.

The arachnid in art, these spinnerets from which . . .
these fragments I have shored . . .
these fractions converted to a failure,
these spinnerets from which issue steeples rotating

and minarets secreted from the abdomen
to enact the casting forth of effort,
to accelerate the casting forth of—
unfortunate minarets

bound in silk and number, not accolade:
"which consists in touching the recipient's cheek with
   one's own"
in touching the recipient with one's own usage,
Modern American Usage,

usage. "Acquiesce," meeting "dream"
on brick, ivy-laden,
ivy in ideological stranglehold,
meaning "assent" or "submit."

To the Finland Station.
Overgrown would suggest nonutility
of disused speech
after years affianced to exile. A figure, stationary

in disbelief. Overgrown would suggest nonutility
"simply by writing the simple word 'not.'"
If not, then not
in varigated stranglehold, overgrown light

and railway ties awash in creosote.
"As a cloud,"
as a cloud now overgrown,
as a cloud now overgrown the recipient's cheek.

Marjorie Welish teaches art history at the Pratt Institute and has taught in poetry workshops at Brown University. Her previous collections include *Handwritten* and *The Windows Flew Open*; her poems have also appeared in such anthologies as *New Directions 54* and *The Best American Poetry 1988*.

The Contemporary Poetry Series
EDITED BY PAUL ZIMMER

The Contemporary Poetry Series
EDITED BY BIN RAMKE